NAILED IT!

Extreme

TRIAL
BIKING

Virginia Loh-Hagan

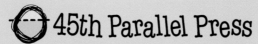
45th Parallel Press

Published in the United States of America by Cherry Lake Publishing
Ann Arbor, Michigan
www.cherrylakepublishing.com

Content Adviser: Liv Williams, Editor, www.iLivExtreme.com
Reading Adviser: Marla Conn, ReadAbility, Inc.
Photo Credits: ©melis/Shutterstock.com, cover, 1; ©Joel Capillaire/Red Bull Content Pool, 5; ©Switn/Red Bull Content Pool, 6; ©Fred Murray / Red Bull Content Pool, 8; ©Mauricio Ramos/ Red Bull Content Pool, 11; © Fred Murray/Red Bull Content Pool, 12; ©Flo Hagena/Red Bull Content Pool, 15; ©Dustin Snipes/Red Bull Content Pool, 17; ©Bill Freeman/Alamy Stock Photo, 19; ©Fred Murray/Red Bull Content Pool, 21; ©Mads Pihl/Red Bull Content Pool, 22; ©jallfree/istock.com, 25; ©MichaelSvoboda/istock.com, 27; ©Joel Capillaire/Red Bull Content Pool, 29; ©Trusjom/Shutterstock.com, multiple interior pages; ©Kues/Shutterstock.com, multiple interior pages

45th Parallel Press is an imprint of Cherry Lake Publishing.

Library of Congress Cataloging-in-Publication Data

Loh-Hagan, Virginia.
  Extreme trial biking / by Virginia Loh-Hagan.
    pages cm. -- (Nailed it!)
  Includes bibliographical references and index.
  ISBN 978-1-63470-485-4 (hardcover) -- ISBN 978-1-63470-545-5 (pdf) -- ISBN 978-1-63470-605-6 (paperback) -- ISBN 978-1-63470-665-0 (ebook)
  1. Bicycle racing--Juvenile literature. 2. Motorcycle racing--Juvenile literature. 3. Obstacle racing--Juvenile literature. 4. Extreme sports--Juvenile literature. I. Title.

GV1049.L65 2016
796.6'2--dc23

                    2015026818

ABOUT THE AUTHOR

Dr. Virginia Loh-Hagan is an author, university professor, former classroom teacher, and curriculum designer. She's one of the few people who has forgotten how to ride a bike. She lives in San Diego with her very tall husband and very naughty dogs. To learn more about her, visit www.virginialoh.com.

Table of Contents

The World as a Playground

Who is Matt Gilman? Who is Andrei Burton? Who is Kenny Belaey? How do they use the world as their playground?

Matt Gilman bounced his bike on one tire. He jumped from a big box. He landed on a smaller box. He reared up on his back wheel. He handles his bike with skill.

Gilman is **blind**. He can't see. But that doesn't stop him. He said, "The first time I got on my bike after I lost my sight, I fell over instantly." He practiced in his living room.

He does trial biking. He does tricks. He uses his city as his playground. He bounces wheels off brick walls. He rides on ledges. He said, "I feel like I can do anything on my bike."

Andrei Burton has been riding since age 13. He's a champion trial rider. He competes in contests. He rides over **obstacles**. Obstacles are objects. He can't touch the ground or obstacles with his hands or feet.

He said, "Trial riding isn't so much about tricks as about riding in different locations. And each place has its

Trial bike riders use the environment as their bike trails.

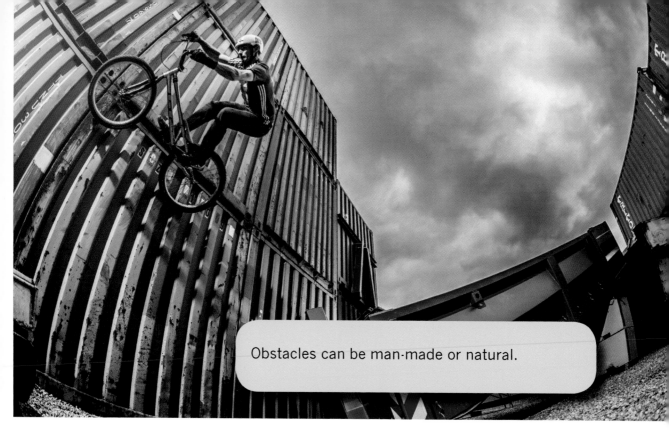

Obstacles can be man-made or natural.

challenges. …I'm always looking for different things to ride on."

Burton had a bad accident. He crashed riding downhill. He broke his hand. He had 16 stitches on his face. He bruised his hip. He keeps riding. He trains more than 35 hours a week.

Kenny Belaey is called "the Magician." He's a champion trial rider. He crashed at a competition. He hurt his wrist. He couldn't ride for several months. He had operations.

He said, "I am still hungry for victories to keep the champion spirit alive." He trained to get better.

NAILED IT!

Spotlight Biography: Thomas Oehler

Thomas Oehler became a trials biking champion at age 17. He's won several competitions. He's from Austria. His father is a rally driver and biker. He started racing on a tricycle at age three. He moved on to trial bikes. He travels the world. He performed bike trials in Kuwait. Several trucks were waiting at a red light. He jumped from truck to truck. He rode his bike on the roofs. He went to the Maldives Islands. He rode his bike on beach rocks, fallen tree branches, and even people. He has set world records. He has the highest bike jump. He jumped 9 feet (2.7 m). He set another record. He jumped over hurdles with his bike. He jumped hurdles for about 1,312 feet (400 m). There were 10 hurdles. They were evenly spaced around the track. He did it in 44.62 seconds. His special talent is "riding technical, tricky lines."

Trials riders perform in all types of places.

His doctors let him ride again. He toured through the United States. He turned a basketball court into his playground. He performed at national basketball games. He performed for 20,000 people. He promoted trial biking. He said, "Just ride your bike every day like it's the last one!"

"I am still hungry for victories to keep the champion spirit alive."

A Thinking Sport

What is trial biking? How is it a "thinking man's sport"?
What are trackstands? What are the two types of trial biking?
What makes trial bikes special?

Trial biking is a type of mountain biking. It's been called a
"thinking man's sport." Riders move through an obstacle
course. They think through their moves. They judge distances.
They bike over obstacles. They must be exact. There's no room
for bad form.

Trial riders ride at low speeds. They learn skills to not touch
the ground. They control their **braking**. Braking is how they
stop. They do **trackstands**. This is when they balance their

feet on the pedals. They can pause between moves. They can control moves. They balance their weight.

There are two types of trial biking. One type is competitions. It's also known as **observed** trials. This means someone is checking the rider. Observers make sure riders don't touch the ground. Organizers create the course. A course must have 14 **trials**, or sections. They have a set time to complete

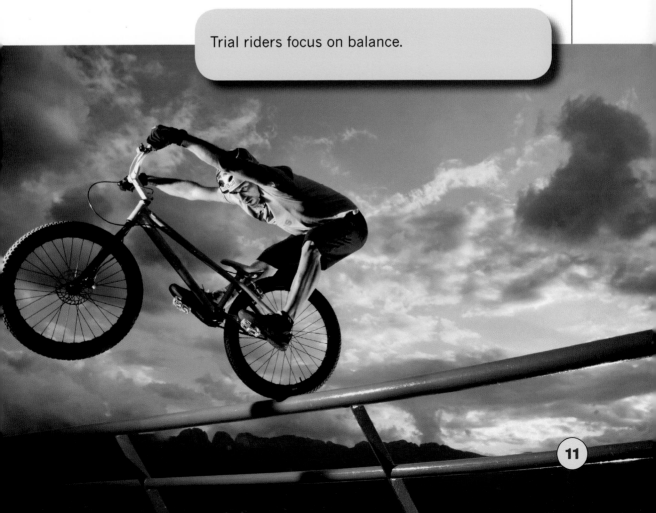

Trial riders focus on balance.

Trial biking courses can have repeating sections.

the course. They get **penalty** points. They get punished for touching the ground.

Another type is street. Street trial riders ride in the city. They also ride in nature. They do more tricks. They spin. They hop. They flip. It's not about winning. It's about controlling the bike. It's about performing.

Advice from the Field: Martyn Ashton

Martyn Ashton is a champion trial bike rider. He also designs trials biking courses. He started by riding motorcycle trials. He was paralyzed during a bike trials event. He misjudged a landing. He fell 10 feet (3 m). He broke his back. He misses trial biking. But he remains positive. He stays involved in the sport. He helps create images and videos about trial biking. He thinks carefully about how to plan tricks. He studies the location. He studies the wind. He said, "There is so much going on behind the scenes on these videos. ... The finished product is supposed to feel really fluid—'oh look, what a great ride, it looks like great fun'—but it isn't. It is six months of really trying to piece things together and create things that just wouldn't be possible normally."

Trial riders have special bikes. These bikes help riders move better. They help riders **accelerate** faster. They need to get going quickly.

They have special frames. They have special brakes. Riders ride while standing up. So these bikes don't have real seats. This makes the bikes lighter.

Trials riders land hard. So their bikes have special tires. A "mod bike" has 20-inch (51 centimeters) tires. This is a **modified** BMX bike. Modified means changed. A "stock bike" has 26-inch (66 cm) tires. This is a mountain bike. A "street trials bike" has 24-inch (61 cm) wheels. This bike is not for competition. It's only for street trials.

"It's not about winning. It's about controlling the bike. It's about performing."

Trials riders make quick moves at low speeds.

From Motorcycles to Bike Trials

How did trial biking develop? Who is Ot Pi? Who is Hans Rey? How did action videos change the sport?

The Pi family developed trial biking. This was in the 1980s. Ot Pi is a champion trials rider. He's from Spain. His father was a champion motorcycle trials rider. He wanted his son to learn motorcycle trials. Motorcycles are dangerous. So they used bikes instead. But Pi loved biking more than motorcycling.

Trial biking started slowly in the United States. Eddy Kessler started by promoting motorcycle trials. He promoted practicing on bikes. It was a great way for kids to learn trials.

He organized bike trials events. He wrote a guidebook for bike trials.

Kevin Norton was the first American to compete in the World Championship. It was in Europe. Norton learned new skills.

Hans Rey moved from Germany to California. He's won many competitions. He's traveled to more than 70 countries. He's been in over 350 magazines. He did many

Many motorcycle trial riders switch to bikes.

Extreme Trial Biking: Know the Lingo

Bacon: scabs on a rider

Beartrap: slipping off a pedal and hitting the pedal with the shinbone

Chunder: crashing

Clean: a perfect ride

Face plant: hitting the ground face-first

Gonzo: dangerous and extreme

Grinder: long, uphill climb

Hammer: riding fast and hard

Honk: throwing up due to being tired from riding

Kack: an injury to the shin received while doing trials

MTB: mountain bike

Potato chip: a wheel that has been badly bent

Skid lid: helmet

Superman: someone who flies over the handlebars and doesn't hit the ground for a while

Tricked out: a bike that has the latest and greatest parts

Wonky: not working correctly

stunts. He **bungee**-jumped with his bike. A bungee is a big, rubber rope. He rode along a 600-foot-high (183 meters) ledge. He rode on ropes down a tall building. He recorded action videos of his stunts. He was the first to do this.

Action videos brought trials biking to a new level. The Internet also changed the sport. Trials riders posted their videos online. This has made trials biking popular. More people practice the sport. Trials riders show off skills. They show off mistakes. They inspire others.

Hans Rey wants to explore the world on his mountain bike.

Danny MacAskill

Who is Danny MacAskill? How did he become a star? What are some of his stunts?

Danny MacAskill worked in a bike repair shop. He spent his free time trial biking around Scotland. He filmed his stunts. He posted the video online. A day later, he was a hit. His video received a few hundred thousand views. He became a star. He's posted many more videos.

He said, "I am very lucky to be one of the first street trials riders to have the opportunity to put all my effort into an online video…. It's a cool feeling to know so many have seen the videos that we have made. And even better that they really enjoyed watching them."

MacAskill is the "king of trials biking." He's been riding since age four. He rode his bike to school. He skidded. He tried popping on one wheel. He rode off big drops. But he needed a better bike. He got a trials bike at age 12. He rode around town. He developed street trials biking.

MacAskill likes challenges. He crashed. He broke his collarbone three times. While he was healing, he studied places. He looked for good paths. He looked for obstacles.

YouTube videos made trials biking popular.

Weather is a challenge for trials riders. It changes their moves.

He said, "I have always looked at the world as a giant playground."

He doesn't let weather stop him. He said, "I normally ride in rain, wind, snow, ice."

MacAskill is not afraid to do scary stunts. He biked on a big boat. The boat floated on the Thames River. It had a 17-foot

That Happened?!?

Fabio Wibmer is known as the "next Danny MacAskill." In fact, MacAskill teaches him. Wibmer said, "Being on Danny's team is still like a big dream for me. As an up-and-coming rider, it is very exciting and awesome to ride with an Internet sensation like Danny, because he was actually the reason why I started trials biking." Wibmer is famous for his big lines and big tricks. He's not afraid to "go big." Wibmer created his own obstacle course. He did it in Osttirol, Austria. It's his hometown. He started by riding along a fence. He made a huge drop. He balanced on his handlebars. He jumped from one bike to another! He continued to ride downhill. He did many more tricks. Just a typical Sunday for Wibmer.

(5 m) loop. He practiced for five weeks. He launched. He made a half circle in the air. He landed on a ramp. He made a loop. He hopped off. He flew over his handlebars. He rolled backward on one wheel. He picked his bike up over his head. People cheered!

He performed many tricks in Argentina. He visited an empty city. It was flooded. He rode up a ramp. He flipped his bike over a sign. He turned a full circle in the air. He landed on his back wheel.

"I have always looked at the world as a giant playground."

Trial riders believe in "flow." They connect tricks, styles, obstacles, and imagination.

Risks and Rescues

How did Danny MacAskill injure himself? How can trial riders reduce risks? What are risks of trial biking on a mountain? What are examples of some rescue efforts?

Danny MacAskill said, "The risks are always there in life. And it really makes you think." He has many injuries from trials biking. He has a pin. It's in his right wrist. He's broken his feet. He's rolled both ankles. He hurt his back. He spends more time hurt or healing than riding. Once, he slipped on goose poop. He hurt his knee.

Accidents happen. Trial riders reduce risks by practicing. They reduce risks by knowing their skill levels. They reduce risks by wearing helmets.

Some trial riders bike on mountains. They can get lost. They can get hurt. A trial rider in the United Kingdom came downhill. He hit a tree. The rider hurt his shoulder. He broke his arm. The rescue team carried him to an **ambulance**. It's an emergency truck. It takes people to the hospital.

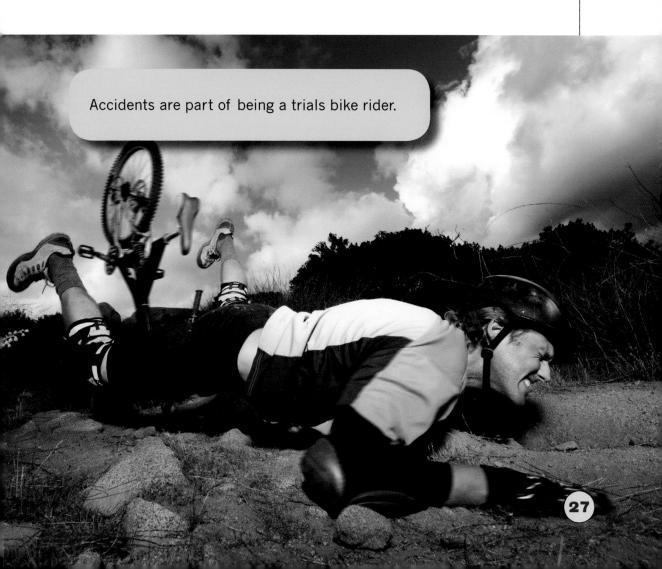

Accidents are part of being a trials bike rider.

When Extreme Is Too Extreme!

Petr Kraus won the trial biking world championship three times. At age 18, he's the youngest rider to do so. He does extreme tricks. He travels around the world. He has biked on glaciers. He rode a skyscraper in Brazil. He rode on a 4-inch-wide (10 cm) wall. He was 29 stories high. He rode up the stairs of a TV tower in Prague. He set a record. He rode 46 floors in 16 minutes and 1 second. He's even biked on a volcano. Pacaya, a volcano, is in Guatemala. It's an active volcano. It erupted violently in 1965. It's been erupting since then. It spews lava, rocks, and ash. It's 8,373 feet (2,552 m) high. Kraus biked on this volcano. He said, "It's amazing to feel this energy from the earth. ... Going down the soft, hot ash field feels like snowboarding in winter."

Going **off-road** can be risky. This is when riders don't use paths. They create their own paths. This can be dangerous on a mountain. England's Buxton Mountain Rescue Team helped a trial rider. The rider was far away. He fell. He broke his ribs. It was dark. The weather was bad. Rescue workers had a hard time. But they found him.

Trials bike riders have fun. But they need to be smart.

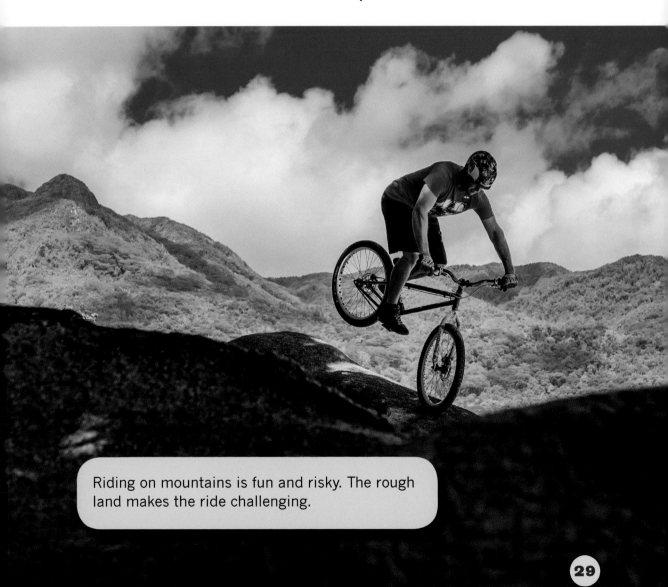

Riding on mountains is fun and risky. The rough land makes the ride challenging.

Did You Know?

- There are different mountain biking sports. They are trial biking, cross-country or trail riding, enduro or all mountain, slopestyle, downhill riding, dirt jumping, free-riding, and pump track.

- Danny MacAskill's dad managed a museum. The museum was dedicated to Angus "Giant" MacAskill. Angus was MacAskill's ancestor. Angus lived in the 1800s. Angus was the world's tallest man. He was 7 feet and 9 inches (236 cm) tall. He weighed almost 500 pounds (227 kilograms). He worked for P. T. Barnum's circus. He lifted horses over fences. He carried 2,200-pound (998 kg) ship anchors.

- Many bikers shave their body hair. Some believe it makes them faster. They fall a lot. Having no body hair makes it easier to scrub off gravel and dirt.

- A professional biker bikes about 25,000 miles (40,234 kilometers) a year. That's like going from Los Angeles to New York City 10 times.

- A human on a bicycle is the most energy-efficient form of transportation in the world.

- Fred A. Birchmore circled the globe in 1935. He biked through Europe, Asia, and the United States. He covered 40,000 miles (64,374 km). He pedaled about 25,000 miles (40,234 km). The rest was traveled by boat. He wore out seven sets of tires.

Consider This!

TAKE A POSITION! There are several different types of mountain biking sports. Trial biking is one of them. Some people believe that trial biking is the most technical. Technical means that it requires a lot of special skills. Do you agree or disagree? Argue your point with reasons and evidence.

SAY WHAT? Street trial biking is like performance art on two wheels. It's been described as parkour on a bike. The Nailed It! series has a book about parkour. Read it to learn more about parkour. Explain how parkour and street trial biking are similar. Explain how they are different.

THINK ABOUT IT! Trial biking came from motorcycle trials. Motorcycle trial riders thought bikes were safer than motorcycles. Learn more about motorcycle trials. In what ways is trial biking safer than motorcycle trials? In what ways is it more dangerous?

SEE A DIFFERENT SIDE! Some people think trial biking is beautiful to watch. They like how riders do tricks on obstacles. Some city officials think trial biking is bad. They think it destroys city property. Why do you think city officials would want to ban trials biking on city property?

Learn More: Resources

PRIMARY SOURCES

Danny MacAskill's *Imaginate*, a Web series about MacAskill's trials biking project, http://imaginate.redbull.com

SECONDARY SOURCES

Mason, Paul. *BMX and Mountain Biking*. Mankato, MN: Capstone Press, 2011.

Osborne, Ian. *Mountain Biking*. Minneapolis: Lerner Publications, 2004.

Weintraub, Aileen. *Mountain Biking*. New York: Children's Press, 2003.

WEB SITES

International Mountain Bicycling Association: https://www.imba.com

USA Cycling Team: www.usacycling.org/mtb/

Glossary

accelerate (ak-SEL-uh-rate) to go faster, to start up

ambulance (AM-byuh-luhns) an emergency vehicle that takes people to the hospital

blind (BLINDE) cannot see; visually impaired

braking (BRAYK-eng) the process of stopping

bungee (BUN-jee) a rubber rope used for jumping off high places

modified (MAH-duh-fyed) changed or altered

observed (uhb-ZURVD) watched, checked

obstacles (AHB-stuh-kuhlz) objects, natural or man-made

off-road (AWF ROHD) going off the regular path, creating a new path

penalty (PEN-uhl-tee) punishment for breaking rules

trackstands (TRAK-standz) a popular trials biking move, balancing the feet on the pedals to keep from touching the ground; helps riders set up the next move

trials (TRYE-uhlz) sections of an obstacle course

Index